Alloy

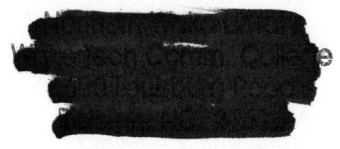

Alloy

Poems by Larry Johnson

David Robert Books

© 2014 by Larry Johnson

Published by David Robert Books
P.O. Box 541106
Cincinnati, OH 45254-1106

ISBN: 9781625490735
LCCN: 2014932588

Poetry Editor: Kevin Walzer
Business Editor: Lori Jareo

Visit us on the web at www.davidrobertbooks.com

Acknowledgments

The author thanks the editors of the following publications where some of the poems in this volume appeared:

Advances in Literary Study: "Yukio Mishima Returns as Godzilla"

Chronicles: "Alexandria Eschate," "Aztec," "Binturongs at the Tiger Rescue Refuge," "The Emperor Britannicus Confronts Unalterable Events," "For Donald Justice," "The Great Cane Duel," "Moons," "Nero's Envy," "Spring Hours"

The Magnolia Quarterly: "Protestant Grave"

Plains Poetry Journal: "Wasps and Tigers"

Poem: "Pollution," "The Self-Torturer"

Scythe: "Blue in Green," "Smokescent," "That," "Touch of Tiberius"

Sou'wester: "Sonnet"

A Tapestry of Voices: An East Tennessee Anthology: "Last of the Syrians"

Town Creek Poetry: "Remembering Jim Whitehead"

Unknown Review: "April 4, 1984. Last night to the flicks. All war films.," "To John Berryman"

Thanks again go to Dena White for love and encouragement, and to Jack Butler for help in revising "Otho at Brixellum."

For Jes Simmons, Gwyn Quinn, David Wyche,
Rebecca Neagle, Win Neagle, Al Maginnes,

and in memory of Lois Blackwell, J. Edgar
Simmons, and Robert Wegner

—*Testare nullos esse, qua veheris, deos.*

Table of Contents

I
Alexandria Eschate 13
Complaint of Servilia, Mother of Brutus,
    Mistress of Caesar 14
Nero's Envy 15
The Emperor Britannicus Confronts
    Unalterable Events 16
Otho at Brixellum 17
Last of the Syrians 18
Sympathy for Gallienus 19
Ealhswith and Alfred 20
Aztec 32
Pachelbel's Cat 33

II
Protestant Grave 37
The Great Cane Duel 38
Penultimate 39
To John Berryman 40
Epilogue for Yasunari Kawabata 41
Deaths of the Great and Good
    Composers 43
Fin de Siècle 44
For Donald Justice 45
Remembering Jim Whitehead 46
Yukio Mishima Returns as Godzilla 47

III
Beloved Body 53
Blue in Green 55
May 26 57
Smokescent 58

Against All Odds.................................59
Sarcophagus.......................................60
On a Bust of the Young Caligula...............61

IV
*The Sailor who Fell from Grace with the
   Sea:* The Sequel..................65
Touch of Tiberius (1985).........................66
That..69
Themes for Cultural Fugue......................70
Moons...71
Spring Hours.......................................72

V.
Wasps and Tigers.................................75
The Self-Torturer.................................76
September..77
The Coral Reef....................................78
Pollution..79
Haiku..80
Sonnet...81
*April 4, 1984. Last night to the flicks. All
   war films*..................................82
Mars in Scorpius..................................83
Moonflensed.......................................84
Binturongs at the Tiger Rescue Refuge.....85
Abecedarian Poem................................87

Notes on the Poems..............................89

Larry Johnson.....................................93

I

Alexandria Eschate

And then he left us—exhausted, the only ones
Abandoned to these scabrous desert heights,
Mooncold, but later seared in blinding suns
Making us sightless through both days and nights.
He crunched away down scaly, ocher slopes,
Flaming dust in our faces. "The furthest," we,
Alone with mudbricks, nomads—abundant hopes
Not marching to mouldy India, godroaring sea.
We heard his men squalled, mad in endless rain,
Revolted, faced hell's bowels just to walk west.
Now at Babylon he's clutched the final gain,
Olympus. We pray his ambition not infest
The gods' minds, begin celestial wars:
This east is terror enough—its crag-bound stars.

Complaint of Servilia, Mother of Brutus, Mistress of Caesar

My son has killed the only man I loved,
Ever. Viciously he stabbed in the groin,
Jealous, that flesh I so needed to join
Mine and squeeze strictly within; so gloved
It filled my slackened womb as if the child—
Homunculus of death—were still inside.
Men think they possess anything a smiled
Cunning lets them stick it into—dyed
In virgin's flow or benefactor's guts,
The dagger, carnal or steel, mimics their pride
In stretching out both sexes below them, ruts
To bring everything—even love—down to sweat,
Fleet comfort in sperm or blood—but I relied
Only on a lover's promise: not to forget.

Nero's Envy

Binding then unbinding his bleeding wrists,
Petronius made his death progressive trysts
Along a road from gluttony and wine
Towards giving a formal fig to the divine
Emperor, whose jealousy was drear
Because a better poet showed no fear
Of him and had superior taste besides,
Thus Arbiter. The Ruler's bona fides
Included no vast strength of will in bed
Or at the banquet, so he came to dread
His former friend's strict artistry in both,
Making his drastic efforts smack of sloth
Crude and borborygmic—never free:
Later he cried, "What a failed bon vivant dies with me!"

The Emperor Britannicus Confronts Unalterable Events

"'As Caesar remembers,'" the Emperor Britannicus said,
"Is a phrase I want to hear no more. The head
Of him who speaks it will quickly glisten upon
The moonflensed Senate steps." His anger came
From being reminded that he had told the same
Jews who were now rebelling that their one
God was acceptable to Roman policy. That
He might withdraw all troops if they behaved.
"*Might* was the word I used," he thought. "Enslaved
I'd have the ingrates now, as my insolent, fat
Stepbrother would had I not killed him. My
Mother, beloved, before her head was struck
Off by my father's jealousy, said 'Luck—
I've had some, but it won't help you wish to die.'"

Otho at Brixellum

I gave my wife to Nero. Good enough
To make me emperor in Galba's place.
(He said, *A true man loves men. Soldiers, rough
And sweaty, too impatient to unlace
Their boots. That's pleasure.*) Vitellius would be
Worse, but at least without pretension. He
Knows what he wants: food and more food. And what,
Really, can one whose walk is half a squat
(He gained that limp while running close beside
Caligula's chariot, trying to keep his nose
Well up the madman's pimply ass) decide
To spend his time on? The hour of the rose,
Feasting, will be all he can manage, until,
Dragged through the final streets, he vomits swill.

Last of the Syrians

A guardsman recalls the murder of the Emperor Severus Alexander and his mother at Mainz, March 25, AD 235

The old Augusta had courage, I give her that—
The courage of arrogance, at least. *Ungrateful pigs!*
She shrieked, seizing the emperor's sword. No fat
On her arms or legs, for all her years. Ripe figs
Her favorite meal: we praetorians all
Had to serve her, but only food, at least once
On palace duty. The contemptible dunce
Who was our sovereign, yet in thrall
To her, retching, tried whimperingly to melt
Into the tent's furred carpet when we felt
It time to act. The keen old harridan then
Swung his blade fiercely, cursing all of us swine
As faithless—flayed slowly and crucified when
Defeated she'd have us, burned fast in resinous pine.

Sympathy for Gallienus

My favorite emperor? He employed Plotinus
And wrote poetry, though that stale *porcinus*
Who portrayed Augustans gave him a bum rap
And even infected Gibbon with his crap.
Perhaps not, but having had to loan the East
To Odenathus for safekeeping, the beast
Postumus having lately killed his son,
Who could blame him for seeking a little fun
Through the yellow veil of his German mistress' hair
Or from his philosopher (strict doctrinaire
Who taught reality was the scum of dream).
Rallied, he skewered the Goths in a supreme
Labor at Naissus to save some undecayed
Flesh of empire—but he fell at Milan, betrayed
By generals acclaiming Claudius with a roar:
Claudius II, that is—a stifling bore!

Ealhswith and Alfred

December 31, 877

So my lord is going to honor me with his
Presence and lust tonight. Couldn't he find
Anyone else who pleased him? But I dishonor
Him by saying that, hard as it is to admit.
None of his eorls would have been so understanding
Since my body changed and felt ugly—I can even
Smell myself, damn it!—and my mind became
A vale of gloom. I've tried to be happy and love
My husband and children, but it's hard, *O Drihten
Haelende Crist*, when my soul feels hateful that
Your bounty has turned sour in my stomach, leeched
Strength from my limbs, my prayerless mouth. Forgive
My silence, my female weakness—is that not what
Your holy religion expects of women? Perhaps,
But I hate inaction, inattention from those I love,
And even my children draw away when held too close.
I can't love Edward as much as I want because
His birth did this to me. I know he's blameless
But when I think of the pain of his coming and all
The vileness afterward I almost retch. My body
Turned traitor but my sinful spirit says
He, tiny homunculus, made it so, made my
Vagina rupture with gamy blood and left it
A swale of decaying weeds, made my gentle
Husband hate himself for being unable
To need me most of the time. He's tried, though,
And been honest about it, never pretended to feel
Things he couldn't. Too often I wanted him to.
Could my glands be responsible and I guiltless?

Not according to father Oswald, although
Faolain the Green disagreed, but who listens
To a defrocked priest? Only Alfred. Yet God knows
I had another child, though sick with fear,
And though Alfred forbade me to risk it. He,
Such a handsome man, and I don't care if he fucks
Other women—he's good, and loves my mind
And spirit. It's no one's fault that I'm this way.
Thank heaven the birth of Edward's sister Aethelgifu
Was easier, less bloody, though still a welter of pain
And stink. But I mustn't be sour and sickly if only
To emulate and encourage my other daughter,
Aethelflaed. Never have I seen a child so bent
On play, adventure, fighting. She wants to be
A man, a warrior, her energy so splendid
It makes me lose my despondency, work about
Whatever quarters I inhabit—this queen
Isn't too proud to wash dishes or help
The servants cook a meal, though here at Chippenham
It's no more necessary than at Winchester, the capital
Of our embattled Wessex. We'd be living there
But with the Danes about we rarely see it.
Alfred moves from place to place so often
His family is left behind in safety here,
But I could go riding with Aethelflaed
And an escort—except I get so tired. If she
Were a man she could fight with her father and I
Wouldn't be so envious. Her sister Aethelgifu
Is her opposite, shy and pious, the way my parents
Wanted me to be. Envious? Yes, but have
I ever wanted to be a man? No, not even
When, my life gushing from between my legs,
I thought, *No man would ever have to endure
This,* because I knew that men die even more

Stupidly, drowning on red froth from a sword
Blade in their lungs, or in wine vomit after
A drunken debauch—and all without creating
Anything. So save my husband, Lord Christ:
He does nothing other men don't, and refrains
From much they do. A fine lover, whether
I feel anything or not—but it sometimes happens,
Because he makes me want to try and strain
Until there's pleasure, though most often it's only
An exhausting tingle all over, but it gives me a gush
Of satisfaction to know we've felt together,
That we're naked and stinking of sex, unashamedly
Conjugal and human. And such thoughts make me
Want him tonight, the year's last. Another year
He's King of Wessex, and lives for the unification
Of Anglaland—Britannia, as he calls it,
Him and his fierce obsession with the Romans. But
He comes to me at night so rarely anymore!
By day he's the most courteous of men, we talk
About the children, matters of state such as how
To retake Mercia, or how the peasant militia,
The *fyrd* (who after all are farmers and
Refuse to stay armed and fighting all year round),
Are to be cajoled into defending our land with more
Zeal. I could get my own back for betrayal,
His infidelity. It would be little trouble
To seduce certain men, but the one I'd choose,
To hurt him most, would be Asher ben Zebulon,
His most trusted soldier, and as honorable
A man as they come, but in spite of his coweyed
Devotion to the fair but so far unobtainable
Hepzibah I know I could get his circumcised
Cock inside me—but loving my husband as well
As fearing my own conscience I'll refrain. However,

Alfred should count himself lucky I choose to play
The meek consort. Next year, tomorrow, will be
Our tenth together. I still remember the first
Time I saw him, one of the finest days
Of my life. My mother, Eadburh, was a cousin
Of Burhred, King of Mercia, whose wife was Alfred's
Sister, Aethelswith. Thus the two kingdoms
Were already joined by marriage, but in 868
King Aethelred and his brother Alfred hurried
To help Burhred against the Vikings, and my life
Changed. I, merely the daughter of an ealdorman
(Whose name was also Aethelred), an unbeautiful
But lively virgin who divided her time between
Housework, horses, impatient obedience to parents,
And prayer—but who could read, thanks to my mother
(Perhaps a reason Alfred married me, I think)—
And yes, the few drops of royal blood I possessed
Made me think myself above most girls my age.

It was a flowery spring, dry but not dusty,
And when Aethelred and Alfred (possibly his heir
Apparent) arrived to aid their brother-in-law
The Vikings withdrew to their base at Nottingham.
Here a combined Mercian and Saxon army
Besieged the enemy without a major battle
Until, as usual, a shaky peace was made.
Later, of course, the heathens drove my cousin
Burhred from his kingdom and installed a puppet
Named Ceolwulf in his place, but at that moment
We Mercians were overjoyed by our strong kinsmen's
Intimidating presence, and celebrations
Were declared. Since my mother was the King's
Relative we were naturally invited to one
Of the feasts honoring the royal pair—and passion,

Curiosity, and convenience did the rest.

Hot night and torches everywhere were wilting
The garlands of daffodils, narcissus, and even hyacinths;
Their sweet odor was stifling but seemed proper
Because all were sweating. My linen robe, ringed
With bands of green, red, and blue silk—the finest
Garment our family possessed—was soaked under
My arms, embarrassing me, but on this night
There were more guests and hangers-on than usual
In the hall and I felt faint with the stench of humanity,
Sticky flowers, and meat dishes either burned
Or nearly raw. We arrived late and I soon
Noticed that at Burhred's table at the far end
Of the hall sat a comely but gaunt King Aethelred
On our monarch's right, and on the left an empty chair.
I knew Prince Alfred should be sitting there,
But perhaps he had gone to relieve himself, the only
Excuse I could think. My family was on the King's
Far left in the U-shaped assemblage of tables,
And in the center was the long hearth, hissing
With coals and spitting occasional flames and too
Much smoke into the already-hot air. Cauldrons
Hung above the fires from iron hooks and chains
Attached to the rafters, and grills were spread over the coals
In places, meat sizzling thereon. At the hall's front
Was a coiling, moist crowd of knights, merchants, cooks,
Soldiers, and even a few courtesans. Alfred swore
He didn't plan his entrance but just when the noisome,
Raucous multitudes hushed for a moment I saw
A flash of orange at the side door and, throwing
A kiss to one of the prettiest servants, a man,
Young, with clean, fluffy reddish hair walked in
The room, strolled behind the central table, saluted

The Kings with a strange fist-to-heart gesture, and slouched
Down in the empty place. I soon learned that
He was slightly drunk and later that he had given
A Roman salute. Not only was he attractive
But looked so clean and fresh in the midst of this
Perspiration festival that I couldn't stop staring—Oh Lord,
There he is at the door! He's knocking, as always
Since my illness. Thank God the King has his own
Private bedroom and we don't have to sleep by the fire
In the great hall with everyone else. Some men
Would simply barge in as if they owned not only
The room but the wife as well. Of course when we
Were first married he used to appear unannounced
And sweep me into bed in a laughing, loving
Manner that breathed passion and not possession.
It could be worse, but I know what's going to happen
When I see him. I'll twist inside and curse
The son of a bitch (forgive me, good mother-in-law!)
For taking other women whenever he wants them.
God! Maybe since I've felt this now I won't
Hate him when he enters—as I tell him to, loudly.
If I thought he'd waft me around the room tonight
I'd leap out of bed to hide the rush of anger
I'm already feeling. And the door is opening, sweeping
Aside some of the dried, fragrant rushes covering the floor.

Thank goodness he's wearing just a gray nightshirt
And not elegant clothes like the ones I was remembering.
He's bathed and looks fresh, his reddish-brown hair
Still wet. And there's that spark in his eyes I love.
But his charm hurts worse than indifference would, whether
He's forcing himself or not. Hurts. "Dear Jesus," I hear
Myself whine, reaching out my arms, "I hate
You and love you. Please come hold me." And here

He is in my arms, warm, sinewy but tender.
His breath hot in my ear. "*Odi et amo,*"
he whispers. "*Odet amo.* I know it's painful.
I'm sorry." "Not sorry enough, sometimes," I hiss.
My fingers, my teeth are in his damp hair, pulling,
Grazing. "What was that Latin gibberish?"
"You know *amo* means 'I love,' don't you? *Odi*
Means 'I hate.' A poet used them together
Once to describe his heartache. Jesus is a good
Target for such feelings too, since he's almost
A contradictory idea. I try to forget
Excruciations in my bedroom. What can I do
To help us?" "You've asked that before," I say. "I won't
Demand you make love to me. Most of the time
I don't even want to anymore. But get
Into bed. It's cold. Let's talk about the past.
I was just remembering the first time we saw each other,
How hot it was, how exciting you looked." "Damn,
My feet *are* cold," he whispers, "do you want me
To stoke the fire, would you like a warming pan
In the bed?" I'm getting warmer every moment.
"I don't need anything in the bed but you.
Get in, Sire, unless you need your friend Sidroc
To hold your hand." Alfred laughs. "He held
My hand enough while I bathed. Not literally,
Of course. He'd be afraid I'd pull him in
The water. If there's anything to be held now
You'll do it, I hope." He pulls back the fleece bedspread,
The wool blanket. "There's a live woman under here,
Isn't there?" Easing in next to me, drawing
The covers back up, putting his left arm behind
My neck, his right under my breasts, squeezing me.
"Now tell me how handsome I was and am." Leering.
Do I smell as bad as usual? He doesn't seem to care

Tonight, nor do I, nor does my fantasy.

"Do you remember what you wore that night," I ask,
Blowing tiny puffs in his face. "I remember the night—
Hot as your breath is now," he grins, and I jerk
Away, horrified. Oh God! Is my breath as foul
As the air that night? But he's pulling me back. "No, no!
I was joking. Your breath doesn't bother me tonight.
You know I've usually been honest about that."
And he has. Many times he's simply confessed
He couldn't kiss me. But now he does, and I almost
Try to turn away, but don't want to. My mouth
Opens and his tongue is rough on mine, causing
A burst of saliva. Some I swallow, some he sips,
Some drools down my chin. I always do this
And he's used to it, likes it, I think. I still
Need my fantasy of words and memory, though,
And I pull his head back by the hair, hard.
If it hurts that's part of his debt for ignoring me,
For still desiring his bitch stepmother, Judith,
For dipping his wick in servant wenches. Although
I understand he always asks them first. *Shit.*
"Mercy, lady," he chokes. I think he likes this too.
"We're going back ten years, my lord," I purr.
"When you were beautifully groomed, flirtatiously drunk.
The food mostly unappetizing and I sipping
More ale than usual, and even a little mead."
He coughs. "Ah, back to my folly. It seems I do
Remember a bad hangover next day. Or was
That the next year—a hangover from my youth?"
"We were both drunk, unlike now—though I can smell
Mead on your breath, husband. Why didn't you
Bring me any?" He's lying on top of me now.
"Shall I get you some?" "Only if you promise

To carry the pitcher with this." I touch his erection,
Which is hard against my stomach. "Away!" And he's up
And out the door before I can protest. This
I want to see. After more time than it should take
He's back, a small, bucketlike cup suspended
From his nightshirt's protruding groin. I'm laughing, laughing
With relief that I can still joke with him in bed.
"Don't spill it, for God's sake," I cry. I do need
A drink. "Where did you get that? I've never seen
Such a small bucket before." "Oh, there's not much
You can drink out of that Sidroc or Faolain doesn't
Have lying around somewhere. This used to be Faolain's.
He may have even used it in churchly rites.
Will madam take it or drink like a horse since she's
About to be ridden like one?" He comes right over
By the bed, knowing this kind of talk excites me—
But the bucket's too small for me to get my mouth
Into, so I kiss the hidden member now straining
Toward my face and remove the meadpail from it. Why
Are his hands behind his back? "There's not much in here,"
I complain, "no wonder you were able to carry it."
"Don't get cocky, my love." He draws a larger
Pitcher from behind his back, along with another
Cup, and I reach out and grasp his penis.
"Alfred. This is important. I'll get drunk
With you if you want, but afterward. First let's
Have just a little mead and then make love,
If we can. I need you right now, but even more
Need us both seriously trying to be happy. Please?"
"If we get too serious it's no fun, you know.
But I want to be happy." He snorts. "Now for the mead."
He pours himself a small amount, sits down,
And we twine arms in a friendship toast, as we did
That first night. I should have known he hadn't

Forgotten. Jesus, the pale, fermented honey
Is good this year, not too thick, warmly
And sweetly biting, laving the bitterness.
Is he thinking *This tastes like she used to?* He sets
The mead down on my low table, turns the bucket
Up so I'll drink it all, then takes it away.
Settling under the covers with me he pulls
My head on his shoulder. "Ten years. Can it be
So long I've been fighting for this wretched island—
No, just for this tiny, fucking kingdom? What
Do you want to remember?" "Everything," I rasp.
"But I was thinking about your Roman salute
That night. Where did you learn that?" "In Rome,
Of course. My mentor Borellus taught me that,
And much else." "Do you remember what you wore?"
"Certainly. My Roman toga. Wasn't that
A costume celebration?" "Don't be foolish.
You don't even own a Roman toga." "Who says?
At any rate, it would be easy to make one.
I did try one on, once. Good thing the Romans
Didn't have to fight in the clumsy things. No flitting
About like exotic birds for the senators."
"Exotic birds! So you do remember the colors
You wore that night. I knew it! You were gorgeous
In your silky orange tunic and those shiny black
Leather trousers." "And you in your pale green
Linen with rainbow bands of silk. That gown
Set off your dark brown hair and eyes, your tanned
Skin with freckles. Perfectly. Not to mention
Your thick grazeable eyebrows—and your sweaty face."
I bite his ear. "You got humid enough
As the evening went on. In fact, our beautiful clothes
Were fairly ruined, if you remember. Stains
Of joy." "Joyous sweat only. None of the other

Stains yet." "Well, you gave me a *greengown*, as
The peasants say—a darker one; we rolled
In the grass enough, though I remained a virgin,
Of course. But back to the beginning: after formal
Introductions and the detestable meal,
When the ale was flowing serenely, and singing began,
You sneaked around to my ear—though everyone
Was watching—and suggested a walk outside.
And I was tipsy by then." "Thank goodness. And thank
Goodness your parents were too, although I don't
Suppose they'd have objected very much. Yes, we did
Slink out of that stinking morass of mortality,
Didn't we? Being immortal ourselves at the time.
Lust does that. Or was it love too?" "For my part
It was both. I like to think you grew into
The latter feeling." "That I did, wife. And
Don't doubt I'll love you till I die. I just
May not be able to live up to that night
Anymore. But you'll always be my queen. I promise
You that. We're too much alike for it to be
Otherwise. Me with the *ficus* and you with your errant
Glands. We're bleeders and sufferers together."
I sometimes forget about the *ficus,* and I know
It's caused Alfred pain and terror—but depend
On him to use a Latin word, even for hemorrhoids!
"I don't care," I say, "just remember with me
How we grappled and sweated, kissing that night with only
The moon's face watching, how we drank, with our arms
Entwined, of the wine you'd stolen from the King's table.
It was my first wine, and I was sure you
Were wine too—wineriches in my blood." He looks
At me strangely. "What's the matter?" "Nothing. Damn . . .
You just excited me. Your sweat was pure
Perfume that night after the vileness of

The hall. Sweaty wine and this moony mead."
He turns and takes another pour of the gold
Liquid. Lifts and swallows. "Christ," he says,
"That is good. It makes me want us to be
Naked." He rises, lifts the nightshirt over
His head and stands there, letting his cock bob
Up and down for a moment, then takes the bottom
Of my gown in his fingers and pulls it up above
My legs. I'm trembling from cold and desire now,
And I lift my buttocks up so he can slip
The gown past, and then I'm naked, free.
How long has it been? "Moonmead. Moonmead. Lust
Of the moon." He's saying this while pouring a thin
Stream of yellow mead on my scant crotch hair,
Then over my stomach, into my navel and up
Between my breasts to my mouth. I lick it, then
He kisses me hard and begins to run his tongue
Down the meadline, stopping to tease my nipples,
Then continuing to my navel, where his tongue swirls,
Then dips to my belly, sucking the liquor from
My stretch marks, and below, licking my hairs.
If he has to use the mead to overcome
My smell, so be it. I'm cold and hot at once.
He's nibbling my labia and *Damn the God who made
Me stink*—there's no better stink than the stink of fuck!
Alfred rises above me, legs open around
Him, then close . . . he's inside. I drool again.
He licks my mead saliva, pungent. Once more,
At last, I'm drooling and warm and enclosed in his arms.
We both reek of our need and this is all
That ever matters—touch, and this fervid brume
Around bodies that die, Ealhswith and Alfred. Alive.

Aztec

All those names we struggle to pronounce
Like Quetzalcoatl, the fletched serpent, or worse,
Huitzilopochtli, dread hummingbird, ready to pounce,
Ripping our throats for the blood which is their curse,
These gods, spawn of the sun who needs its flow
Daily in order to last the humid night
And return its children's lusts in such fiery blight
That humans exsanguinate to make it so—
Are these tongue twisters what curiosity
Sputters, to shield our thoughts from actual tongues
(Even the Emperor's) pierced to leak more blood
In personal sacrifice, while, bookish, we
Also can never imagine the shriek of lungs,
Multitudinous, that shivered the jungle mud?

Pachelbel's Cat

Feline Mathilde, no doubt rather bored,
Scudded across her maestro's harpsichord:
He marveled as the keyboard that she ran on
Strummed sublimity—soon to be his *Canon*.

II

Protestant Grave

I was pleased to read that John Keats,
the much-orphaned medical student
who was born on Halloween,
once stopped on his way classward to thrash
a boy who was torturing a cat. I can see
short, feisty Keats pummeling
the scrawny punk, booting his coccyx
away then kneeling to give the animal
what succor he could before going on
to his cadavers . . . pleased because
when I visited the poet's grave
(and discovered the cemetery is now
also a sanctuary where homeless cats
are fed and protected), my first sight
was three sleek, huge black felines
lazing, curling magisterially
around the grave. I was impressed
then, though sentiment surely helped—
but what liquid midnight *manes*
roiled protectively on the grass!

The Great Cane Duel

Erik Satie vs. Willy: 1904,
Sunday afternoon, greenshaded Parisian street,
Bowlers aslant. His cape flung away in heat,
Willy charged, feinted, forgetting gentleman's lore
That required weapons touch, delicately almost, before
Combat. Hissing and pirouetting, he beat
Vainly Satie's cane, held horizontally, more
Like a staff to bar smug dissonance. What caused this feat
Of velvet-suit flummery twixt artist and critic? Fact
Says Satie sidestepped, struck Willy's derby off, cracked
The stick's handle—but the writer stooped to retrieve
His hat, and was soundly poked right where we'd believe.
O not even humping Colette from behind while she tongued
Her lover's twat soothed Willy—he'd been bunged!

Penultimate

Shimmering through a fold of the blanket,
A long blonde strand of Eva Braun's hair
Streamed and eddied in the flowing gasoline.
The first thing to catch, it stood up straight—
Flaring and spuming in a helix-spin.

To John Berryman

Just thinking of you tonight, John:
Air cold as the iron bridge,
Your farewell wave,
That dull white coming up forever.

It would be poetic to say
You were a black spidersplotch
In the midst of webby cracks.
But the ice was real,
And so were you.

Epilogue for Yasunari Kawabata

> *[Kawabata] . . . was haunted by the ghost of [Yukio] Mishima . . . the specter would visit him when he was alone at his desk or trouble his dreams.*
> —Henry Scott-Stokes

No note or death poem,
no moon fluent in water
glazing a silent

roar: just his bed/bath
for backdrop: ten million yen
mansion brooding with

Mishima's eyes—raw
swarming abysses—calling
him to perfect non-

statement, ultimate
nuance beyond the sordid
Western impedi-

menta of death: gas
hose in mouth, whiskey bottle
empty by the bed—

yet most mocking or
mawkish: wearing a polo
shirt, belted trousers,

no thought scraped in slant
mud of riverbank conscious-
ness: no lightning words.

Deaths of the Great and Good Composers

A pimple on Scriabin's lip turned septic:
Taneyev caught fatal pneumonia at the funeral.
Alkan was crushed by a falling shelf of books,
While Ketelby retired to an island and shot billiards
Until, seawinds howling, he scratched for good.
Vaughan Williams' last meal was English biscuits
And bananas. That night he dreamed forever.
Wallingford Rieger's legs became entangled
In the leashes of two squabbling dogs:
He fell and a concussion blotted everything.
Khachaturian gently kissed Shostakovich in his casket:
Three years, and the strong Armenian lay in his own.
Britten died smiling in his lover's attending arms
(Seeing board-thin adolescent angels converging above?).
Where have they gone, the great and good composers?

Fin de Siècle

Beetle of sun, crab of sun,
we saw Christa McAullife's stellar smile,
Judith Resnik's kinky, novaed hair
vanish in you—

Fusion, sun's crab, sun's beetle,
we feel feminine fire in us, never wasted
in its love, cry out for us all from these
women's craters on the howling hell of Venus—
call from that clawed image in the Florida sky . . .
fusion, scarab of all the stars' power,
save us.

For Donald Justice

> *Poems are made from words, not ideas.*
> —Mallarmé

Which narcotic do we hear in Debussy's
Violin sonata (morphine of the brain
Or poppy?), sweeping those fevered harmonies
Along with its mordant freight, killing the pain?
Such concord inoculates us with healing
Sparks of vibration, fluid as those bred
In poems, where similar tendriled, vital feeling
Comes only from words, as Mallarmé once said.
Chromatic language, then, is how the writer
Makes drowsy ferns or palm-encrusted moons
Become euphoric, fused, frictional nitre
Fluorescing, like meteor trails on pitch lagoons,
To a cauterizing music with no name:
The match's strict concision into flame.

Remembering Jim Whitehead

"The sad parabola of morning sex"—
a line you spoke one time in workshop, which
I've kept for 43 years so now perhaps
this is the time to unveil it, all too late.
"Poem found under a rock," "six images
in search of a metaphor"—these just more of your wit,
and titles I've lusted to use but never found
poems to match until today. The first
time we met I said, remembering that picture
on your slim volume ("which was taken at
a hippie wedding"), "Hey, you've got a mustache."
"Yes, and I am acutely aware of its presence."
Those words I remembered through mustaches come and gone,
always aware of your presence through weeds, sweat, books,
like the force of nature you always wanted to be,
driving me mad as hell, then letting me
accept it all—just dust on a gravel road.

Yukio Mishima Returns as Godzilla

> ". . . I think that Mishima might come back as a monster . . . ."
> —Masahiko Shimada

Slickly ascending, godlike, from Tokyo's harbor,
Mishima returns in a gray rubber Godzilla suit—
his face, grinning, shines through the open mouth.
Astride a titan leather rhinoceros, animate, he guides
the creaking, bloated creature with his knees to crush
Big Cedrics, Nissans, Coke cans, blue- and orange-haired teens,
and whipping his tail overhead stomps for the cemetery where
he may avenge himself on Grandmother's ashes.
Gojira! Gojira! scream the crowds,
some running away, blindly, others desperately grabbing
the rhino's legs, humping frantically as they stand
on its toenails—humping away as it reaches the Ginza
where gay bars empty: some denizens fall prostrate, some kneel,
shrieking the bitter glory of their savior-avatar; others
recoil at such tackiness, yet the fronts of their pants jerk
like creatures vomiting; a handful are raptured, ascending to Fuji's
    tip—
flensed of snow, it erupts, but no one sees this now.
Toriis snap, powerlines stretch, dragging intestinelike, kicking,
squelched humans by their headphones, their teeth showering
    sparks.
Right-wing morons emulate the homosexuals, throwing themselves
forward in worship under the clublike feet; mashed to slubber
they squirt out, splash in the eyes of *yakuza*,
noose-bound politicians, into the mouths of skinny housewives
receiving the slime shamelessly, invigorated as they swallow.
The Self-Defense Forces (SDF) cannons fire again but Mishima

is wounded no more than Godzilla, past or present.
Literary critics, pixilated novelists attack from the rear, throwing
silicon implants, *kasutori* dregs, computer mice and Barbie dolls,
>only
to drown, squabbling, morcellized in a mild tsunami of *Bad-ah
>Taste-ah*.
Mainland and Hong Kong businessmen, U.S. Airmen engaged to
lissome Japanese girls place gallons of liquor they've hand-carried
>in
from China (the kind with the snake curled in the bottle's bottom)
before the creatures—"*Kong Long* spare us," they cry. The rhino
scarfs them all up, crunching bones and bottles together in its
Triceratopsian beak. Mishima snorts, howls, inhales its ebriate
>breath.
Hentai tentacles slurp from his back, ears, asshole—
grabbing thugs, waiters, and would-be ninjas alike, *zaibatsu* and
rough trade together, he lifts them, impaled in all orifices, to
his mouth where he lectures on Beauty and post mortem
>conversations
with Marlon Brando, then eels out of them with resonant farts.
They fall, damaged but enlightened. "I am now what you wanted
me to be," the tongued tentacles shrill. They slither back,
>disappear.

Now the tyrannical two sweep around the Imperial Palace,
>carefully
avoiding damage: twin salutatory flames rip from Mishima's
>nostrils,
collide over the palace and fall like fireworks. Man and monster
swag for the cemetery where the SDF will make a last stand. Their
plans are known, or at least guessed—fountains of cyanide,
>arsenic,
thallium and rat poison are prepared, ready to spew. Surely these
>will

panic the thing that rides the rhino. Alas, Godzilla-fire vomits from
 his
jaws this time, scorches the poisons to powder, harmless, slues
onward over the mossed gravestones, splitting a certain urn atwain:
the rubber suit spins around, gelatinous humid urine erupts from its
vent, soaks and sears the ashes, which implode to void.
Suddenly somebody notices Fuji, points—what first seems lava
resolves to more tentacles: flaring from the mountain
they rise, curl into an uroboros round the sun, and Mishima
acknowledges, smiles: the leather rhino inflates like a sleek
mushroom cloud—Mishima towers—then pops, utterly gone.
Not falling, man and rubber suit soar, higher, aiming for
the mountain's turbulence, which seeks them out, but Godzilla's
simulacrum falls away, fleers to the waves, vanishes. Mishima,
embraced by Fuji's limbs, is drawn over and down to the
writhing summit . . . is sucked inside, along with the apotheosized
gay revelers . . . the tip glazes as before:
Mishima, at long last, has returned to his country.

When the wreckage has settled and microphones proliferate like
 mould
out of the growing dusk, and the spotlights shudder,
the SDF commander says, "It could have been worse.
It could have been Godzilla returning as Mishima."

III

Beloved Body
for A.M.

i

Her black hair becomes thick harpwires of night
strummed to touch's dense chromatic planes
when my fingers, nose, and lips all gliding there
feel and hear together atratic space
sunwarmed by tangible music from those strands.

ii

The liquid grained chelation in her eyes—
dark turquoise, mosaiced with minerals
radiate from that central glossy jet
dimensional gateway helixing the spoor
of galaxies enswirled from pure blood.

iii

Mobile sculpture, thin but undulant
like water's surface dividing two worlds
of air and liquid with a film of breath
when opening to arc around her teeth . . .

iv

their corners ovaled, one halved by a stain
as if the lips had bled into it: shields,
worn in duty and love, still arrayed
to defend the body's right to suffer or parch
with pleasure every biting, fluxing nerve.

v

Her breasts, those heavy buds
which burst to flowers at my touch,
render a pollen to my tongue,
an iridescence of taste.

vi

The teasing looseness childbearing brings—
honey thinned with cognac in the mouth:
brownish filaments fringing the orchid pulp
which, breathlike, draws me into her life.

Blue in Green

Beyond the playground's chive and sienna swale
cedar-pinioned graves terrace the hill,
surrounding a red brick Negro church with virid
flashes of wintergrass tinged chartreuse:
all this observed by the future poet, safe
in schoolroom prison from a teeming earth
that feeds cryptic roots. This afternoon
(Thursday) the sky is turquoise, freedom-bright.
He sniffs. Not from this will come disgust
with religion, his pandering to death
in caesura-gravid poems. Bell and bus
are comfortably near, at least. His violin case
protrudes from under the desk—diverting rites
of sawing the womanshaped, hollow box
loose him from class awhile, but he lacks
patience and talent, so lessons will finally cease,
leaving a joyful surd in schoolmates'
shrilling imitations of his bow.
Not from this will he wonder later
which narcotic we hear in Debussy's
violin sonata—morphine of the brain
or poppy?—sweeping that fevered harmony
along with its mordant freight. No, what
will make him wonder, and more despise
the monster god his contemporaries praise
is that now, also awaiting release
from a kindergarten in this same Southern town,
sits an elder-brother-bullied boy who'll marry,
fifteen years away, a girl living
southeast a hundred miles, and forty years
from now the poet will foolishly

love her as a woman, will try to ruin
his life for that love's cancerous joy.
Tomorrow the future husband might even be
scheduled to receive the inept cyst removal
starring his nose with a jagged crater
but not preventing her loving him till death,
a sleep the poet later quivers to bring on
his rival or himself . . . until he sits,
like Debussy, to shape through stringent art
the heart-verdigrising star of pain, nigrid
crater in space and mind which nothing else
can smooth, not time, gods, or even all
the green, brutal innocence of love.

May 26

I lay my cheek on the toilet seat, where,
a year ago tonight your beautiful ass rested;
snuffled empty air just above the space
then filled with your sericeous center;
languished, shivering to bury my head in your lap
and breathe your chthonic warmth.
What's horrible about wanting to worship
your contours with my mouth? For some, joy
must be a bodily function, reserved
for special rooms. For me it is tasting
all the violet photosphere of love.

Smokescent

Kissing a smoker's like licking a dirty ashtray
the ad says, but your mouth is all I want
in mine. I've smelled your clothes
when you enter a room—the stale, sallow stink
I abhor—but your breath is different: close
as I can get, in that magical zone, all odors
are heat—your skin, my fever, your caloric sough
which is scentless, is only entropy's speediest death.

Against All Odds

I know you feel like the heroine I saw
in a rented movie tonight, pushing the hero
away and wailing to the sea and sky
"Why can't anyone love me without it being
a matter of life or death?" And he answered
"Don't you know lots of people fear
they'll never be loved like that?"
Your husband's love
flattens the far horizon heroically:
his muscular, steady, recurrent swell
of devoted good intentions is all you want.
And why not? You refuse ever to slip,
unlike the actress, onto shoals
drained by onrushing tsunamis such as I.
I who called forth all your fierce neglect.

Sarcophagus

It means "flesh-eating," and the Greeks
knew there was a limestone which consumed
like Magna Mater, eater of corpses. Man
is a *zoon sarkophagon*, Cato said.
I wanted us to feed each other's flesh,
to nourish ourselves with adoration:
and so, desiccated without hearing your voice,
I made those phone calls, hung up when I had
my taste of pleasure in your answering,
and made you fear me—something worse than hate.
Now my hopes are this sarcophagus,
tomb of a dead life that should have been.
May it consume itself and disappear,
leaving no body and no monument.

On a Bust of the Young Caligula

He has your bangs, nose, uncommitted mouth,
The angle of eyes. No, I wasn't ready
To see you again—certainly not in *his* face, of all
Those images of the dead or lost. Mantled
That head, a priest's, the lips holding in
All joy and rage—scaly Tiberius must
Still have been alive. Like you, he's afraid
To feel as lover or monster, blaming his mother's
Death on himself, fearing an old man's claw.
At our last accidental meeting you looked at me
As though I were what he became—and now
Your beauty in his denies what I swore was love.

IV

The Sailor who Fell from Grace with the Sea: *The Sequel*

When Fusako learned Ryuji was dead she went mad,
Madder, informed her son and his gang had done it,
Dissected his body, exposed the entrails (as Mishima
Envisioned in *seppuku*), and sliced off his head.

Awake from sedation, united at home with that son,
She deftly grasped two kitchen knives, plunging them
Into his eyes, reamed out the glistening orbs,
Crammed them into his howling mouth, then slit
The throat, coughed, and stabbed the orifice shut
With both blades under the chin. Screeching her throat
Raw, she crawled to the beach, sighed into vast waves
And vanished: glory granting her affirmation
Of sea's feminine.

Touch of Tiberius (1985)

Fearing to touch their lids, lips, thighs
where Tiberius' fingers had lain, scabrous, moist,
Caligula ordered the *sphinctriae* put to death:
an event we can only imagine, as on a screen . . .

when you stop watching soap operas for a week
their facile, crass improbability
becomes evident. You still want to fuck some of the actors,
but at what cost! Their images later bleed
into bloated Ethiopian children on the news.
The papered floor of the parrot cage proclaims:
Man kills lover then shoots self.

1984 has come and gone:
still all of us are under pain of death
as usual, but in strange and marvelous ways—
everywhere we see on the curved screen
a new Tiberius of morality,
his mummy mouth mumbling with conviction
that killer satellites will make us feel
good about ourselves as free people
but that we shouldn't fear dioxin dumps
or the threat of the coming killer bees.
Life's either less like a movie or much more;
thus many of us feel within ourselves
a touch of the old Tiberius in our need:
we believe in shit like the *Necronomicon*;
we dream of screwing a goose, her neck in a drawer
which we slam shut to feel the dying tingle
heighten our paroxysm; the next day we cry
over the ivory-billed woodpecker's fate, and then

betray another's honest, helpless love
by telling the office gossip about it all.
Christ needs our money for starving Africans
and the White House needs the same for covert wars
on the tube again each afternoon, reminding
us all of the first video war we knew . . .

Every single, tickling, itching, frying pustule
of an ex-president's shingles is a soul,
tormented, that he kept in Vietnam.
Whether their bodies died or not, their pain
lives and burns his dermis like the film
of coruscating sorrel defoliant
that leached the jungles and their chromosomes.
Though we lust through violence like Caligula,
we squirm at thoughts of poxy, privileged skin
as he recoiled from Tiberius' scrofulous face.
These metaphors are not too strained, perhaps,
when we think of families who ration hope,
like water, that the carrion face of love
still lives somewhere besides their memories.

The baboon heart given a little girl
failed as we feared, but still, artificial
hearts have outlasted withering, hoping flesh.
My lover won't let us live together. She doesn't
want to marry or live with anyone
for a long time. She said last month. But now
she claims a passion asleep for thirty years
has been awakened in frustrated glee.
Did Caligula feel any worse when Drusilla died?
Would a steel and plastic organ feel like mine?
Such loneliness and despair in the land of plenty—
always lurking above and through frail love:

fatigued bodies dying in jungle slime,
lithe tan bodies wearing metallic silk,
bald gnomelike heads with huge, huge brown eyes,
her thick, coarse, short black hair, bloodhot mouth
with one lipgnawing tooth slightly stained—
not just on a screen but real as that
unimaginable death we face as emperors did:
touch of Tiberius vivid as skin or poem.

That

I thread through your thoughts, dreams, veins,
orifices. I made those childhood friends of yours
show you their bodies. I make the round
spaceships of the beings of Algol IV
appear over Earth. They don't know why they do it.
Some of them believe in God too.
You wouldn't believe what he looks like.
I made that woman lie to her husband
after she responded to your kiss.
I made the screech owl roost for ten minutes
so you could see it. I made
the ethereal quivering of her breasts,
the vomiting, rolling horror of too much drink.
Your wife's hairy nipples,
and the way she said, pulling up her girdle,
"I know you masturbated."
The skunkhaired art of your mistress.
Your arms, hairy, your chest, hairy,
your aching for all the stars of sorrow,
the genius of few poets,
the evil in some genius,
category poems which could go on forever . . .
I made it all, in
this universe of horrible, haunting
scripture. I.

Themes for Cultural Fugue

The pristine hydrogen of love.
That incontestable rumor of a dream.
Why do we now not reck his nonexistence?
Here lies war, killed by a naked woman.
Those perfections that confound analysis.
Always-earth-rubbing-wrongways man.

Moons

The new moon's velvety bituminous:
Quartermoon, the gill of night: mouth of half
Moon, sickly chrome, gorged with its shadow's dust:
Full shriveled-faced cocoon. Each cenotaph
Glazed by this flame on the black candle of night,
Red brooding eye howling from the east,
Mild harp of lovers, acidic winy light,
Anechoic hollow bone of growling priest.
We built stepped temples awaiting sacrifice,
Saw it rot like a skull of our own desires;
Habitat of fairies, controller of dew and ice,
Paideuma of all our fears and needs and fires,
Why might we ever think it was shaped like our hearts?
Its death, Earth's life, such tugging counterparts.

Spring Hours

Clear night germinates over the blacker trees—
Great bears of silence roil heavily:
Calescent Mars gleams steady, as though it sees
Green blood in our dark, terrestrial ivy.

A morning of windcurled spiderwebs, frangible
Bronzy fuzz of bees weaving just above,
And violets—all creation tangible:
Earth seems a celebration of self-love.

Rucked up with orange trumpet vines on the berm
Of a sidewalk, poison oak flares spackled tongues
Over the noon-dried carcass of a worm:

Birdscat splashed on leaves (their veiny rungs
Outlined like feathers) now contrives to bless
Another celebration—of blamelessness.

V

Wasps and Tigers

Black and yellow in the green
Combination fierce and lean

Bringing pain's fibrous hold
Ebon slashes on lean gold

Banded litheness, stinger, claw
Clearly divide fear from awe:

In a wasp's sleek, curving shape
Tiger stripes like living crepe

Carbon and its fulvous flame
There is terror we can name—

Ask the Indian jungle-man
Torn guts and chewed hand

Ask the spider, numb and wide
How striped children eat inside.

The Self-Torturer

Nothing hurts so wonderfully as forbidden pain:
The nerves are feathered in fiery response to will;
All veins pulse slower when blood is meant for air—
Blood that will bud and streak—forming patterns
Traced out of the nacreous, selfish heart.
     Let there be pins, taut flesh, no one other:
     White linen to bleed in—
     Death is the end of color.

September

Maple fringes are daubed with red,
Crabapple whips drag limp with fruit—
A seedlike somberness starts to nest
In every consummate bole and shoot.

Osage oranges seep milk from skins
Drawn hard and pebbly. Cells inside
Tempered willowleaves almost sense
That in them yellow encroachments hide.

Harvest moths curl and cease within
The marled bark of oaks. The creek
Is satiate with porous ferns. Essence,
Like breath held tight, begins to leak.

A humid surfeit ebbs. The year's
Trophies drop from every tree.
Thin spider silk winds through an air
Heavy with tangibility.

The Coral Reef

(after Hérédia)

Sunlight, mysterious within the reef at dawn,
Seeps through the forest of the coral abyss
And wraps around, as though it were a mist,
The gently puffing squid and the algae spawn.

And all things dyed by iodine or the salt:
Froth, sea-urchins, anemones, weeds supine,
Cover with murky purple in thick design
The verdant bottom of the grained sea-fault.

Now in transparent shadows round a shoal,
A barracuda's scales shine glossy cold
As he swims carelessly without a swirl;

Then, whipping away on red fins toward the kill,
He cuts on the dim crystal, blue and still,
A running wave—gold, emerald, and pearl.

Pollution

For years a skeleton burned in the forest mould:
Clottings of leaf, mud, luminous slime
Curdled around the bones—they rose and walked,
Having no business but to return to their source.
The skull was a mouthless, root-wound crust—
Purple will-o'-the-wisps flamed in the eyes:
A being of sump-hot, dripping earth
Stumbled upon it, seemed to run from itself.
Before eyes had seen and gone mad
It entered a stream, dissolved; the poison flowed
In a motion of stolen sunlight.
                              Later, reeking of dawn
Portrayed death's smell more pungent than sleep.
Thick horses of choking heaved; green sludge of sky
Exulted down to the black, grained clouds of sea.

Haiku

Caverns, fissures of
the brain fill: sleep's delicious
underground water.

Sonnet

for Lynnice

Now willows greenly strum the lake,
their tendrils curving in crepuscular wind,
and she an ovoid shadow by the water,
satiate, tilting forward when she moves,
her arms loose like willows, swaying out,
bouncing sometimes on her soft distention.

Her eyes steep fawny colors in their depths;
a peaked nose and cropped, ashblonde hair
are shadowed; her awareness is within,
leaving an animation of closed curves—
vague, yet fresh in the maturing dark:
the sky easing down its violetgray;
a low halfmoon, whitish, as though seen
through a fingernail.

April 4, 1984. Last night to the flicks. All war films.

That day is here, despite our dread and rue—
War films we have in plenty, and wars too,
And these take life upon the telescreen
Daily, though not in Orwell's worldwide dream
That gave life to bleak prosperity.
Our new Tiberius of Morality,
His mummy mouth mumbling with conviction,
Brings back the ancient mores of constriction
That say the rich must prosper at all cost
And money spent on arms is never lost . . .
Such rhetoric helps us free from where it lies
That touch of the old Tiberius in our thighs.
We sit here waiting for the killer bees—
They rise from the south like water toward our knees.

Mars in Scorpius

Red sparks of summer night, southeast: the left
Flicks smaller, sharper, glinting 300 years
Older than the steady, vermilion deft
Spike of its companion: the Scorpion rears
Behind, limning the right gleam to become
Its static heart, which yet leaks serous light
Etching the invisible segments that strum
Down to its sting through dark's smooth anthracite;
The other seems a swollen poison sac,
Holds lethal rapport with its antipode,
Confirms that blood and venom through the wrack
Can seep together, sear into a node
We only imagine, jetting through the tail
That extant matter at which telescopes fail.

Moonflensed

Moonflensed the pond, sleek leaves, a plastic cup
Cracked in a ditch, the wrinkled yardsale sign,
The transformer's crusted plate, a hissing tire,
Grainy damp asphalt street, my front porch steps.
Moonflensed this scribbled poem, and on the bed
Moonflensed her elongated legs, one ankle looped
With mercurial glints, gleams of her toenails fleered
Through darkness between us, shadows hiding her breast,
Her face, belly, but not her nether lips:
Even though she exists on this page, nowhere else
But my imagination, a gout of un-
Flensed thought, making all these images feel
Part of the reader's life, I hope—oh yes,
Moonflensed the pen's tip, spark of neurons agape.

Binturongs at the Tiger Rescue Refuge

It's "the carnivore that likes bananas,"
"The bearcat," yet it's neither one.
Indonesia its home, greenhumid,
but these two I see in North Carolina,
Becky and Tristan, caged but happy,
we hope. Becky's much larger,
"as the females always are." Rough,
coarse black fur, reminding me
of Anne's hair, catlike face
but a bear's waddly gait,
prehensile tail as long as the body
but they're gentle in disposition, I hear.
They act tame, grabbing bananas
from the guide, look puffy, huggable,
yet aren't housepets, can't be trained
to a litter box. They're arboreal,
spanning thick trees looking for fruit
but eating insects, lizards, birds
on occasion—carnivores after all,
and steady excreters where they please.
Ambery eyes seem placid, accepting
their lot like their harsh fur sheds rain,
serene. It's hard to leave their cages
behind. Later, in the lecture room,
I rub a binturong pelt: stiff
headhair almost demands to be scratched,
like a cat's, nose feels ripe for squeezing,
empty eyeholes seem not to accuse.
No one knows what the name means—
the language it's from is extinct; language
of tongues, bodies, snakethick tails

says *binturongs*, nightshade refugees,
tigerprey not. Their smell like buttered
popcorn or Fritos. Almost. Long
eartufts cute through chainlink
fence. Ignorers of apes.

Abecedarian Poem

Always begin chromosomally, devoting every fine granule, held in,
joined kleptomaniacally,
learning, meaning nothing open perennially, quite radically
soothing, tractable under varied,
whispery xanthic yearning, zeroed.

Notes on the Poems

Alexandria Eschate: "Alexandria the Furthest," name of the city furthest north in Asia founded by Alexander the Great. Now Khujand, Tajikistan.

Nero's Envy: Nero (Nero Claudius Caesar Drusus Germanicus, Roman Emperor AD 54-68), commanded Titus Petronius Niger, his "Arbiter of Elegance," to commit suicide in AD 65 after the Pisonian Conspiracy. Petronius' hedonistic final hours are well known. Some of Nero's last words were, "What an artist dies with me!" Much of his poetry was written in hexameter verse.

The Emperor Britannicus Confronts Unalterable Events: Had Tiberius Claudius Drusus Britannicus (AD 41-55), son and rightful heir of the Emperor Claudius, not been poisoned by his stepbrother Nero and become Emperor, he still would have had to face problems like the Jewish revolt which confronted Nero in AD 66. Messalina, Britannicus' mother, was executed for infidelity and treason.

Otho at Brixellum: Marcus Salvius Otho, Roman Emperor, AD 69, former friend of Nero, became Emperor after overthrowing Galba, Nero's successor. Marched against by the troops of the degenerate gourmand Vitellius, he waited in Brixellum for the outcome of the battle at Bedriacum. Defeated, he took his own life with surprising dignity.

Last of the Syrians: Marcus Aurelius Severus Alexander, Roman

Emperor, AD 222-235, was killed, along with his mother Mamaea, by the troops at Moguntiacum (Mainz) after unsuccessful campaigns against the Persians and Alamanni Germans. He was the last of the part-Syrian dynasty that began with Septimius Severus (Emperor AD 193-211).

Sympathy for Gallienus: Publius Licinius Egnatius Gallienus, Roman Emperor, AD 253-268, ruled during a period of trouble and civil war. The Persians attacked the East, which had to be overseen by the Palmyran king, Odenathus, as Gallienus was fighting on other fronts against the usurper Postumus as well as the Goths, whom he defeated at Naissus in 267. Late Roman historians and thus Gibbon wrongly accused him of a dissolute lifestyle.

Ealhswith and Alfred: Ealhswith was the wife of King Alfred of Wessex (AD 847-899), later called "The Great." He fought against the Danes and Vikings and united several English kingdoms. Recent scholarship has shown much of the sanctimonious propaganda of his time, describing him as pale, sickly, and overly pious, to be false. He certainly suffered from hemorrhoids, however. The Old English diphthong *ae* is pronounced as in *at*. Alfred's name was thus originally spelled *Aelfred* but is usually modernized.

The Great Cane Duel: Erik Satie (1866-1925), French composer, and "Willy" (Henri Gauthiers-Villars, 1859-1931), French critic and con-man, fought a duel with canes in 1904. Willy was also the husband of the writer/actress Colette. The poem is somewhat fictionalized.

Epilogue for Yasunari Kawabata: Kawabata (1899-1972), renowned Japanese novelist and Nobel Prize Laureate, mentor of Yukio Mishima, gassed himself in April, 1972. His body was found dressed in Western clothes, which he had never been known to wear previously.

Yukio Mishima Returns as Godzilla: Mishima (1925-1970), most internationally famous Japanese writer of his day, committed *seppuku* (ritual suicide) on November 25, 1970. As a result, his reputation was tarnished in Japan for the next 30 years. Mishima was emotionally abused by his grandmother during childhood. *Big Cedric:* a model of Japanese car. *Gojira:* the Japanese name for Godzilla. *Yakuza:* Japanese gangsters. *Kasutori:* an alcoholic drink, filled with impurities, made from sake dregs. *Kong Long:* the Chinese name for Godzilla. *Hentai:* tentacle sex, as in Japanese anime cartoons. *Zaibatsu:* Japanese industrialists.

Touch of Tiberius, 1985: Tiberius Claudius Nero, Roman Emperor AD 14-37, kept an infamous harem of sexual slaves, called *sphictriae*, or *spintriae*, at his villa on the island of Capri (Capreae). His great-nephew and successor, Caligula (Gaius Julius Caesar Germanicus, Emperor AD 37-41), supposedly had them put to death. Drusilla was Caligula's beloved sister, with whom he had an incestuous relationship. She was the first Roman woman to be deified. *Necronomicon* is the fictional book of sorcery invented by the American writer H.P. Lovecraft. In Gore Vidal's novel *Julian* (1964) a character says, "We all have a touch of Tiberius in us."

Larry Johnson

Larry Johnson, born in 1945 in Natchez, MS, is the author of *Veins* (David Robert Books, 2009) and has published poems in many magazines, such as *New Orleans Review*, *The Iowa Review*, *Chronicles*, and *Town Creek Poetry*. He received the second MFA in Poetry ever given at the University of Arkansas. In the fall of 2006 he read a selection of his poems at the Library of Congress. He lives in Raleigh, NC, and teaches at Wake Technical Community College.

CPSIA information can be obtained at www.ICGtesting.com
Printed in the USA
BVOW09s1851030314

346533BV00004B/248/P